Pulleys

by Joanne Mattern

BELLWETHER MEDIA • MINNEAPOLIS, MN

BLASTOFF!
2
READERS

Note to Librarians, Teachers, and Parents:

Blastoff! Readers are carefully developed by literacy experts and combine standards-based content with developmentally appropriate text.

Level 1 provides the most support through repetition of high-frequency words, light text, predictable sentence patterns, and strong visual support.

Level 2 offers early readers a bit more challenge through varied simple sentences, increased text load, and less repetition of high-frequency words.

Level 3 advances early-fluent readers toward fluency through increased text and concept load, less reliance on visuals, longer sentences, and more literary language.

Level 4 builds reading stamina by providing more text per page, increased use of punctuation, greater variation in sentence patterns, and increasingly challenging vocabulary.

Level 5 encourages children to move from "learning to read" to "reading to learn" by providing even more text, varied writing styles, and less familiar topics.

Whichever book is right for your reader, Blastoff! Readers are the perfect books to build confidence and encourage a love of reading that will last a lifetime!

This edition first published in 2020 by Bellwether Media, Inc.

No part of this publication may be reproduced in whole or in part without written permission of the publisher. For information regarding permission, write to Bellwether Media, Inc., Attention: Permissions Department, 6012 Blue Circle Drive, Minnetonka, MN 55343.

Library of Congress Cataloging-in-Publication Data

Names: Mattern, Joanne, 1963- author.
Title: Pulleys / by Joanne Mattern.
Description: Minneapolis, MN : Bellwether Media, Inc., 2020. | Series: Blastoff! Readers: Simple Machines Fun! | Includes bibliographical references and index. | Audience: 5-8. | Audience: K to grade 3.
Identifiers: LCCN 2018056034 (print) | LCCN 2018060219 (ebook) | ISBN 9781618915337 (ebook) | ISBN 9781626179936 (hardcover : alk. paper)
Subjects: LCSH: Pulleys--Juvenile literature.
Classification: LCC TJ1103 (ebook) | LCC TJ1103 .M36 2020 (print) | DDC 621.8/2--dc23
LC record available at https://lccn.loc.gov/2018056034

Editor: Christina Leaf   Designer: Jeffrey Kollock

Printed in the United States of America, North Mankato, MN.

Table of Contents

Have you ever
opened window blinds?
You have used a pulley!

Pulleys help people raise and lower objects. They can lift heavy **loads**.

pulley

load

Pulleys have three parts.
A wheel turns on an axle.
A rope sits on the wheel.

axle

wheel

groove

Many pulleys have
grooves on the wheel.
These hold the rope in place.

How Do Pulleys Work?

Pull down on one end of the rope. That **force** turns the wheel, which lifts the load.

Lifting the load is easier because it is easier to pull down than to push up.

How Pulleys Work

pulley

rope

load

downward force

upward force

Make a Pulley!

- a bucket with a handle
- some heavy books
- an empty paper towel roll
- a broomstick
- several feet of rope

What To Do:

1. Fill the bucket with books. Try to lift it. It is heavy!

2. Tie a rope around the bucket's handle.

3. Place the broomstick through the paper towel roll. Lay the rope over the roll. This is your pulley.

4. Have one person hold the broomstick. Have a second person pull the rope over the roll to lift the bucket. Is it easier to lift now?

One pulley alone changes
the force's direction.
But it does not take away
force needed. Sometimes an
object is still too heavy.

Adding more pulleys makes lifting easier. It takes half as much force to lift the same weight with two pulleys instead of one.

Compound Pulley

A compound pulley is two or more pulleys working together. Try adding a pulley to the one you made in the first experiment.

What You Need:

- a door handle
- a second paper towel roll
- the pulley from page 10
- another long-handled broom or stick

What To Do:

1. Untie the rope from the bucket and tie it to the door handle.

2. Place the broom handle and paper towel roll pulley through the bucket's handle.

3. Slide the second paper towel roll over the other broom handle.

4. Have someone hold the second broom.

5. Take the rope and bring it under the first paper towel roll and over the second.

6. Pull the rope downward. Is it easier to lift the bucket using two pulleys?

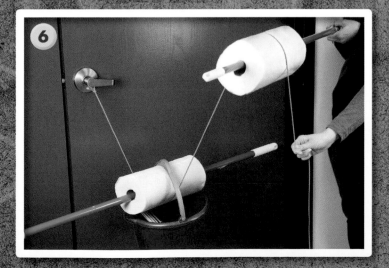

More pulleys need more rope. The force must be spread out over a longer **distance**.

How Compound Pulleys Work

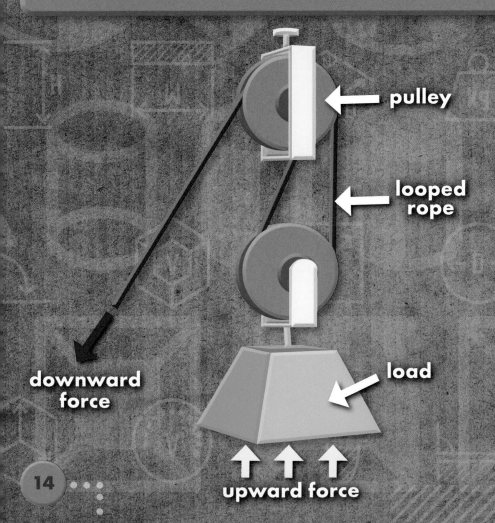

pulley

looped rope

downward force

load

upward force

compound pulley system

This makes up for using less **effort**.

Pulleys in Our Lives

Long ago, people used pulleys to build castles. Pulleys lifted heavy stones.

Pulleys also raised **drawbridges**.

pulley

drawbridge

We still use pulleys today!
Pulleys raise flags high up
on flagpoles.

pulley

harness

Some pulleys lift construction workers to their jobs. A pulley hooks onto the worker's **harness**.

pulley

lever

Pulleys are part of
complex machines.
A crane uses a pulley
to lift things.

Everyday Pulleys

Simple

flagpoles

curtain pulls

Complex

elevators

bicycles

The crane's arm is a **lever**.
Pulleys help get the job done!

Glossary

complex machines—machines that combine two or more simple machines

distance—the space between things

drawbridges—bridges that can be raised so that people cannot cross

effort—energy that is used to do something

force—energy that has an effect on something

grooves—long, skinny cuts that keep an object in place

harness—a set of straps worn around the body

lever—a simple machine that turns on a point to help with lifting

loads—objects that are moved or lifted

To Learn More

AT THE LIBRARY

Dickmann, Nancy. *Pulleys.* Tucson, Ariz.:
Brown Bear Books, 2018.

Lee, Mi-ae. *Use a Pulley!* Minneapolis, Minn.:
Lerner Publishing Group, 2016.

Rivera, Andrea. *Pulleys.* Minneapolis, Minn.:
Abdo Zoom, 2017.

ON THE WEB

FACTSURFER

Factsurfer.com gives you
a safe, fun way to find
more information.

1. Go to www.factsurfer.com.

2. Enter "pulleys" into the search box
   and click 🔍.

3. Select your book cover to see a list
   of related web sites.

Index

The images in this book are reproduced through the courtesy of: Fotofermer, front cover; Yuliya Evstratenko, pp. 4-5; guilermo_celano, p. 5; Nordroden, p. 6; jayk67, pp. 6-7; Oliver Hitchen, pp. 8-9; Bellwether Media, pp. 10, 13; Feylite, p. 11; Kim Christensen, p. 12; Canaran, pp. 14-15; Prisma Archivo/ Alamy, p. 16; aaabbbccc, pp. 16-17; Cassiohabib, p. 18; King Ropes Access, pp. 18-19; Phatr, pp. 20-21; hxdbzxy, p. 21 (flagpoles), Ashley Aslett, p. 21 (curtain pull); Rachi Jalayanadeja, p. 21 (elevator); Rafal Olkis, p. 21 (bicycle).